keepers

by alice schertle · illustrated by ted rand

lothrop, lee & shepard books

new york

Monopoly

From the hilltop you can see
the city, like Monopoly,
laid out on a paper board.

Little pieces far below,
plastic houses row on row,
holding little plastic folk
asking how the game is scored.

Little unseen plastic folk
driving through the city smoke,
following the boulevards,
taking chances,
taking cards,
driving all across the board
asking how the game is scored.

Little busy businesses
laid out on the streets below,
waiting for the plastic folk
driving through the city smoke,
driving cars with little wheels,
moving forward, making deals:
Boardwalk,
Park Place,
passing Go,
Reading Railroad,
B & O,

moving all across the board
asking how the game is scored.

A fir tree leaning
over the water drops a
pine cone on the moon

Water drips from a
yellow umbrella lying
open in the hall

As I bury my nose
in its pink petals the
rose begins to buzz

The thin shadow of
a fox slides across the wall
of the chicken coop

Carousel

Mine, the black one, rears on his hind legs, plunging
forward, lunging after the others: lions,
palominos prance in a swirling circle,
dancing around us.

Falling, rising, falling again forever
spinning, holding tight to the bright brass pole, I'm
laughing, singing, stroking my horse's polished
ebony shoulder.

People watching swim past my vision, waving;
I'm the leader, others come leaping after,
we are swept along in the sound of organ
music and laughter.

Last Patch of Snow

Under the woodpile
all alone,
hunkered down
in a shadowy zone,
ear pressed
to the chinks
between the logs,
Winter hears
the bees and frogs
and cicadas sing,
and Winter thinks,

"So this is spring!"

May is

May is
loud with mother
and father birds hopping
up and down, hollering, *"You can
DO it!"*

Walk Softly

Walk softly
in this wood,
where little wispy things
in gown and hood
slide down the dark
and fold their wings.

Shy and hidden
shadow things
of pipe and ring
and strange remembered power.
Shadow voices
high and thin
quiver in the wind
this witching hour.

Little fragile fading things
turn watchful eyes
upon me as I pass—
a sudden rustle in the grass
as something flees
before my awful
bone and blood.
Walk softly
in this wood.

The Better Beetle

A beetle climbed a hollyhock
growing in the ground;
when he reached the very top
he looked around.

He peered down from a flower
on his brother bugs below
and saw that he was far above
the other bugs, and so,

having climbed much higher
than his sisters and his brothers,
wasn't he a better beetle
than the others?

"Look at ME, look at ME!"
he shouted. *"You'll see*
I'm a whole lot higher than you!
I can tell you from here
it seems perfectly clear
that you have to look up to me, too!
Pay attention, you ninnies,
you weaklings, you skinnies,"
he cried. *"I've climbed to the top!*
Look at me now, bugs,
you earwigs, you sowbugs—
The Beetle That Nothing Can Stop!
Whoever refuses
to climb up here, too, is
a groundling. . . .a coward. . . .I hate him!"

As he shouted and waved
his antennae and raved,
a woodpecker flew down and ate him.

A Frog in a Well
Explains the World

The world is round
and deep
and cool.
The bottom of the world's
a pool
with just enough room
for a frog alone.
The walls of the world
are of stone on stone.
At the top of the world,
when I look up high,
I can see a star
in a little round sky.

Spider

Spider
in your mansion airy:
Patience!
It will not be very
long
before a fly unwary
blunders
in.

With your
tender
touch
you'll tap him.
Lovingly
in gauze you'll wrap him.
And with any luck
you'll trap
his next of kin.

Keeper

My father taught me
how to cast
and let the line out slow
and taught me how
to wait. And how to know,
at last, when something
took the bait.
I set the hook by
jerking on the rod and
finally dragged my fish
aboard. His round eye
had a startled look. He
gulped the painful air.
I worked the metal from
his lip, and with my finger
stroked his head
and wished that I could slip
him overboard,
but didn't dare.

"This one's a keeper, Son,"
my father said.

The Worst Day

Today,
the first dry leaf,
the first
      back-to-school
      flat tire
      blue Monday
      smog alert
      no dessert
      strike out
dry leaf
      fell
      down
      dead—
Made a crater
as big
as my head
on the lawn.

Summer
is
gone.

After School

After school

the sun
put his
hot hand
on my head and
      leaned
on me
all
the way

home.

I, Alone: a Riddle

Forgotten
among the rubber bands
and thumb tacks,
I have admired
the thin transparent tongue
of the tape, envied
the metal jaw
and sharp silver teeth
of the stapler.
I roll modestly to the back
when you open the drawer,
but I, alone, can open
the round white eye
of the flashlight.

Folder

Covered
with a blanket
of dust, last year's three-ring
folder dozes under the bed
dreaming

of hot
pink indexes,
crisp manila pockets,
sheet upon sheet of fresh, wide-ruled
paper. . .

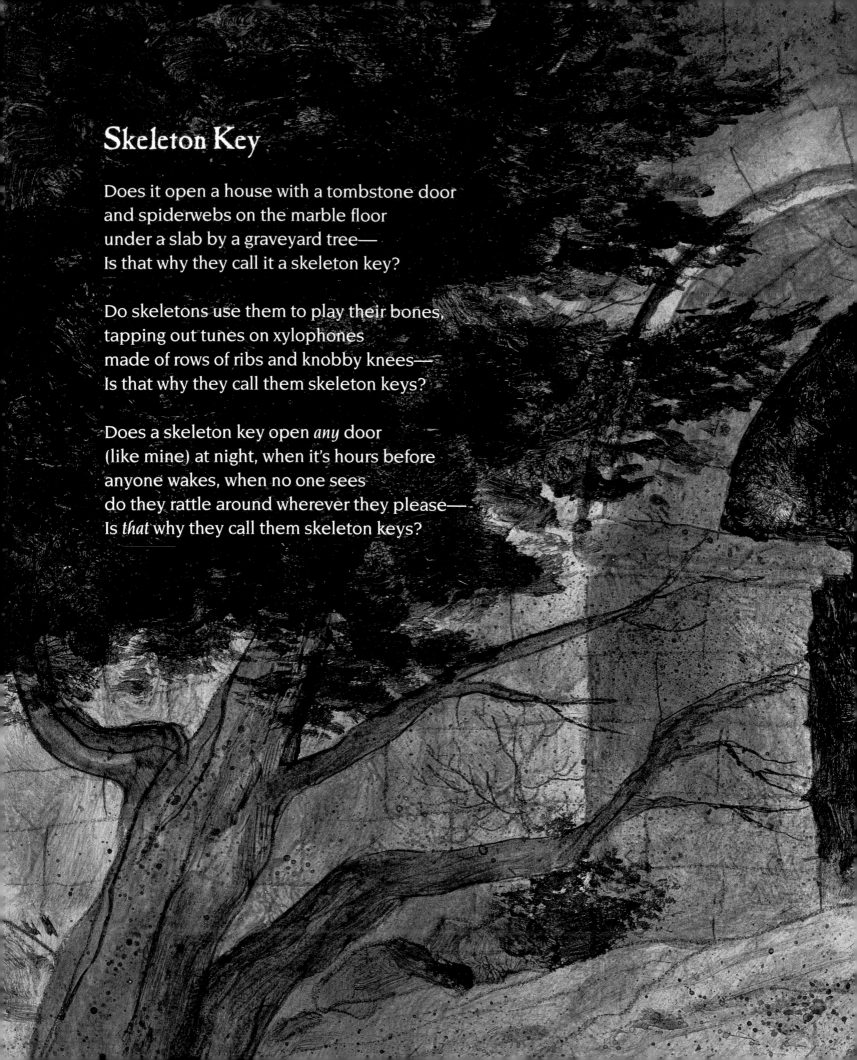

Skeleton Key

Does it open a house with a tombstone door
and spiderwebs on the marble floor
under a slab by a graveyard tree—
Is that why they call it a skeleton key?

Do skeletons use them to play their bones,
tapping out tunes on xylophones
made of rows of ribs and knobby knees—
Is that why they call them skeleton keys?

Does a skeleton key open *any* door
(like mine) at night, when it's hours before
anyone wakes, when no one sees
do they rattle around wherever they please—
Is *that* why they call them skeleton keys?

Slow Steps

There,
in the dust,
he burst his seams
and slipped his sequined skin.
I place my slow steps
through the grass
and wonder if
he passed
thissss
way.

Lizard

Athletic
lizard,
looking trim,
sun glinting
on the scaly skin
stretched tautly
down his
tapered
waist
comes out
to taste
the fresh air
of the fall,
and do his thirty
push-ups
on the
wall.

Galleon

She rests upon her starboard side.
Little silver fishes slide
between her ribs, and in her hold,
where tentacles embrace her gold,
a curious current gently stirs
the round white bones of mariners.

Bristlecone

I stood in a forest
a thousand years or so.
Was it two?

Ring on ring
the heart of me grew.

Winter on winter
my branches have borne
their burdens of snow.

Around me the others have fallen.

The weight of my winters
has twisted and tightened
its grip on my spine.

Withered, whitened,
alone I survive,
a bone on a hill.

Alive.

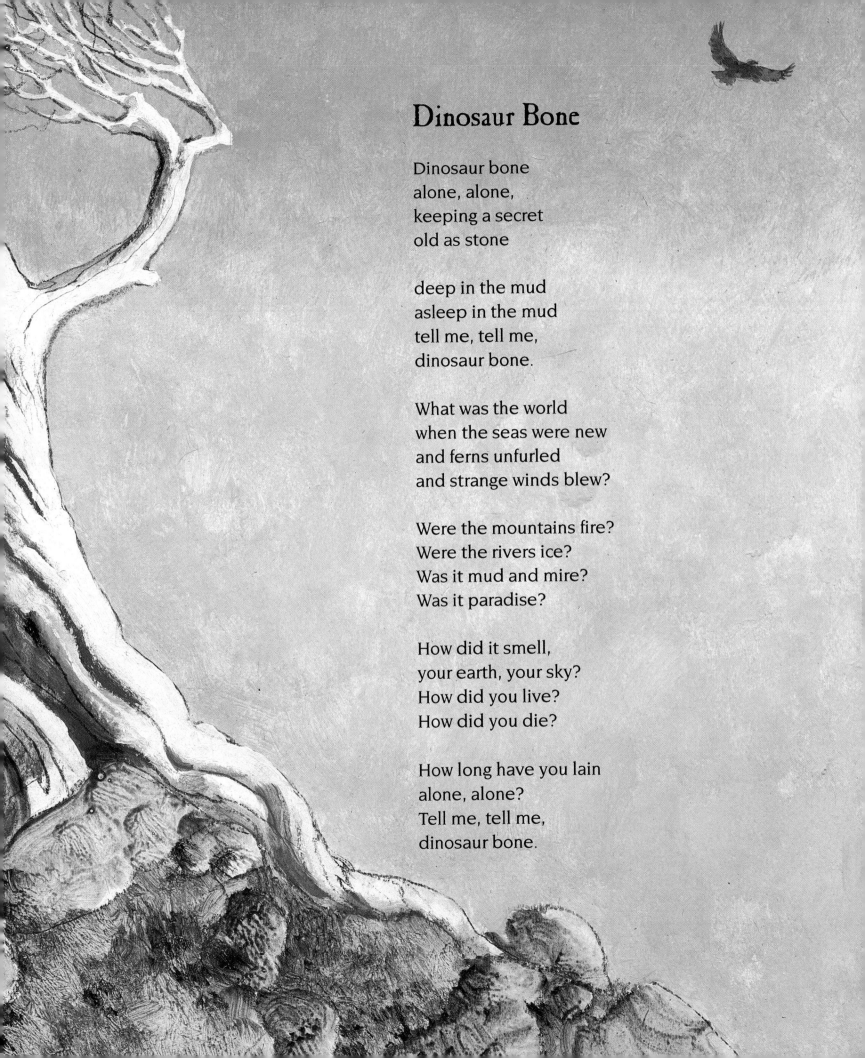

Dinosaur Bone

Dinosaur bone
alone, alone,
keeping a secret
old as stone

deep in the mud
asleep in the mud
tell me, tell me,
dinosaur bone.

What was the world
when the seas were new
and ferns unfurled
and strange winds blew?

Were the mountains fire?
Were the rivers ice?
Was it mud and mire?
Was it paradise?

How did it smell,
your earth, your sky?
How did you live?
How did you die?

How long have you lain
alone, alone?
Tell me, tell me,
dinosaur bone.

A Silver Trapeze

A silver trapeze of my own: I dream of it nightly.
A slim silver bar at the end of a rope I seize
and am lifted, carried, I'm flying above the ground lightly.
A silver trapeze.

Down and around and up on the crest of a breeze
I swoop, I soar through a cloud, hesitate slightly,
then loop the loop like a pinwheel and hang from my knees.

Up through space I race on a bar shining brightly,
touch the tip of a star whenever I please,
kick off from the moon, sweep soundlessly down, holding tightly
a silver trapeze.

My Old Dog

My old dog
doesn't move much
anymore.
He's stretched out on the floor;
I hear him snore
a time or two.

He's done his share
of chasing cats and cars
and barking strangers
at the door.

Now he likes it best
to rest
here on the floor,
his muzzle on my shoe.

Ukelele

My father bought me a ukelele
when I was seven,
and taught me how to play the chords
and taught me how to sing the words
to *Avalon* and *Chinatown* and *My Blue Heaven*
when I was seven.

I'd strum like anything
and we would sing *My Wild Irish Rose*—
I still know how it goes—and
Ain't She Sweet and *Whispering*,
and then my dad would tune a string
and take a turn with something new
and he would say,
"They don't write songs like that one anymore!"
and I was sure that it was true.

I think one day I broke some strings
and didn't bother putting new ones on.
And I went on to other things,
the way kids do.

And if I had a uke today,
I don't suppose that I could
play the thing at all.
But I know how to sing the words
to *Darktown Strutter's Ball*,
and *Don't Bring Me Posies*,
and *Mandalay*, and *Rosalie*,
just the way my father taught me
on the uke
my father bought me.

to Melanie Donovan, my friend who quotes poetry
—A.S.

for Bill Martin, Jr.
—T.R.

Text copyright © 1996 by Alice Schertle

Illustrations copyright © 1996 by Ted Rand

Printed in the United States of America

First Edition   1 2 3 4 5 6 7 8 9 10

Library of Congress Cataloging in Publication Data

Schertle, Alice. Keepers / by Alice Schertle; illustrated by Ted Rand.

p.   cm.   Summary: A collection of poems including "Last Patch of Snow,"

"A Frog in a Well Explains the World," and "My Old Dog."

ISBN 0-688-11634-5. — ISBN 0-688-11635-3 (lib. bdg.)

1. Children's poetry, American. [1. American poetry.] I. Rand, Ted, ill. II. Title. PS3569.C48435K44 1996 811'.54—dc20

96-3702 CIP AC

The answer to "I, Alone: a Riddle" is a battery.